The Vegan Teen Cookbook

Easy vegan meals from what's already in your kitchen.

Cathy Hutchison

For John...
Much of who I am is because you believe in me.

For Brooke and vegan teens everywhere...
Your compassion is inspiring. It matters.

Living Vegan.

As a vegan in your teens, you are as passionate as your adult counterparts, but you are often working with limitations that adults don't face. Limited income stream, lack of transportation, living counter-culturally within your own family...

It can make living vegan a challenge.

This book is about being able to cook for yourself. To live out your convictions without having to continually compromise or defend your stance. (Because if your family sees you living and eating well, they will stop worrying or thinking you might change your mind...well, at least a little.)

This book is your idea guide to:

- Make a meal.

- Pack a snack.

- Learn new stuff.

- Eat out.

- Have the conversation.

With that said, let's get started...

Make a meal.

We all need to eat. And while our lives would be easier if we each had our own personal vegan chef, for most of us that isn't an option. As a vegan teen, you need simple things that you can make with items from a regular grocery store.

Every meal in this section is laid out on a grid, giving you options so that you can customize each meal based on whatever your parents happen to already have in the pantry or refrigerator. Simply pick one entry from each column and mix/match according to what you have on hand and your personal taste.

If you haven't cooked much before, let's go over a little recipe shorthand...

> 1 t = 1 teaspoon

> 1 T = 1 tablespoon

That's it! So, pick a flavor and let's go.

Tex Mex

Most people think of meat and cheese when they think of Tex-Mex, but the real flavor is in the spices and textures.

Choose a Base	**Rice** *Prepared according to package directions*	**Tortilla Chips**	**Corn or Flour Tortillas** *Make sure the brand you get uses vegetable oils instead of lard.*
Make a Filling	Heat 2T of oil in a skillet with ¼ c diced onion and sauté in		
	Chopped Veggies Whatever you have on hand like zucchini, bell pepper, green chilies , mushrooms, yellow squash, carrots, or broccoli	**1 can of Lentils** (drained and rinsed) **+ 2 t taco seasoning**	**1 can of Black Beans** (drained and rinsed) **+ 1 cup Frozen Corn**
Choose Some Toppings	**Sliced Avocado**	**Diced Tomato**	**Sliced Black Olives**
	Shredded Lettuce	**Lime Wedges, Diced Onion and Cilantro**	**Salsa**

Soft tacos made with corn tortillas and lentil filling, topped with lettuce, tomato, lime, onion and cilantro. Time from idea to table? 15 minutes.

Italian

The flavor in Italian food comes from olive oil and fresh garlic.

Choose a Base	**Bowtie Pasta or Rotini** *Prepare according to package directions*	**Spaghetti or Linguini** *Prepare according to package directions*	**Pizza Crust** *Bake in the oven after topping with sauce and other ingredients. Buy premade or find a video on how to make from scratch. Tortillas or pitas work in a pinch.*
Create the sauce	Heat 2T of olive oil in a skillet with 1 clove sliced fresh garlic and sauté in		
	1 28 oz Can of Crushed tomatoes and 1 T Italian Seasoning	**1 can of Cannellini or other White Beans** (drained and rinsed) **+ 2 cups Spinach** (fresh, frozen or canned, drained)	**Sliced Mushrooms + 2 T cooking wine + 2 T soy sauce**
Choose Some Toppings	**Sliced Peperoncini Peppers**	**Fresh Chopped Herbs**	**Sliced Black Olives**
	Capers	**Red Pepper Flakes**	**Artichoke Hearts**

Linguini topped with White Beans and Spinach with Red Pepper Flakes: Time from idea to table? 30 minutes. (It takes a while for water to boil.)

Asian Stir Fry

For Asian dishes, vegetables are typically cut into bite size pieces and cooked at high heat for a short amount of time.

	Soba or Rice Noodles	White or Brown Rice	Ramen Noodles
Choose a Base	*These can usually be found on the Asian aisle in your grocery store. Prepare according to package directions.*	*Prepared according to package directions. Or get a small rice cooker. They are affordable and speed up the process.*	*Prepare noodles according to package directions. Toss the flavor packet, it is probably not vegan.*

	Heat 2T of olive oil in a skillet with 1 clove fresh garlic and 1 t minced ginger root or ¼ t ginger powder and sauté in		
Stir Fry Some Veggies	**Broccoli cut into small Pieces or Package of Broccoli Slaw Mix** *(sold in package in produce section)* **+ Sliced Mushrooms**	**Water Chestnuts, Bamboo Shoots, Sliced Carrots, Sliced Celery and Bell Pepper**	**Package of Frozen Stir Fried Veggies**
	To spice it up, add a dash of dried red pepper flakes, a sliced jalapeño, or a dash of Sriacha sauce to the vegetables while cooking.		

	When the vegetables or tofu are almost done, mix together the following in a separate bowl then pour into the wok or skillet over the stir fry and cook for 1 – 2 minutes longer		
Make a Sauce	**1 c vegetable broth mixed with 2 t cornstarch and 2 T soy sauce**	**½ c vegetable broth mixed with 2 t cornstarch, 2 T Balsamic vinegar and 2 T soy sauce**	**2 T cooking wine 2 T soy sauce 2 T maple syrup**

Note that you can also buy premade Asian sauces at the grocery store. Try Thai peanut sauce, Hoisin sauce or a simple teriyaki.

Asian stir fry made from broccoli slaw with mushrooms and jalapeño added. Served over white rice. Time from idea to table? 20 minutes.

Indian Curry

Curry is made by heating aromatics like onion and garlic in oil along with spices, then allowing the ingredients to cook in their own juices. The result is a stew-like dish that is served over rice or with flatbread like naan.

Choose a Base	**Flatbread** *If naan isn't sold in your grocery store try heating a flour tortilla or pita in the oven until the edges get crisp.*	**White or Basmati Rice** *Prepared according to package directions*	**Crackers or Pita Chips** *Non-traditional, but not bad if that's what you have to work with.*
Create the curry base	Heat 2T of oil in a pan and add diced onion or several cloves of fresh garlic, sliced. When the onions have cooked until clear, add a sliced tomato and one of the spice sets below		
	1 T Curry Paste (any kind)	**1 t garam masala** **½ t chili powder** **½ t ginger powder** **½ t turmeric**	**½ t turmeric** **½ t chili powder** **1 t coriander** **¼ t ground cumin**
Add the main ingredient	**1 can Garbanzo Beans, drained and rinsed**	**1 cup chopped cauliflower and 1 potato peeled and diced**	**1 package frozen mixed vegetables or 1 - 2 cups of whatever veggies you happen to have on hand**
	Continue on low-medium heat stirring occasionally until vegetables are the desired consistency. The vegetables should provide enough juice to cook in, but if it looks like the curry is too dry, add ¼ a cup of water.		

Garbanzo bean curry made with onion, sliced tomato and curry paste. Served over brown rice made in a rice cooker. Time from idea to table? 30 minutes.

Sandwiches

Sandwiches have not traditionally been vegan; however, with some imagination, you can change that.

Choose a Base	Hoagie or other Sandwich Roll	2 Slices of Toast	Pita
Choose a Filling	**Sliced Avocado + Tomatoes**	**Garbanzo Bean Salad** *Mash a can of garbanzo beans with a potato masher and add mustard, diced onions, diced celery, salt/pepper and lemon juice to taste.*	**Black Bean Patty** *Usually found in freezer section. Microwave according to package directions.*
	Falafel *Prepare according to package directions.*	**Peanut Butter + Sliced Bananas**	**Grilled or Sautéed Vegetables**
Choose Some Toppings	**Lettuce**	**Sliced Tomato**	**Salsa**
	Grilled Onions	**Maple Syrup**	**Tahini Dressing or Vinaigrette Dressing**

Kaiser roll filled with grilled onions, tomato, avocado and lettuce. Paul Newman's Olive Oil and Vinegar dressing gives it more of a submarine sandwich taste. You could also try a deli mustard. Time from idea to table? Depends on the filling, but usually 5 to 15 minutes.

Soup

The best part about soup is that it is really cozy when it is rainy or cold outside. It also makes a light lunch that won't weigh you down when you are active.

Choose a Base	**1 carton Vegetable Broth** *Or less if you want less soup.*	**1 large can of tomato or V-8 juice** *Or less if you want less soup.*	**1 carton onion soup** *Read the ingredients to confirm there are only vegetables.*
	Put base in a stock pot and bring to a low boil.		
Put Stuff in	**Diced potatoes**	**Bag of frozen mixed vegetables**	**Garbanzo, Black or Kidney Beans** *The canned version...rinsed and drained.*
	Sautéed onions and Sliced green apples cooked in a separate pot in 2 T oil until they are caramelized.	**1 can lentils,** **+ Sauteed diced onion,** **+ sliced carrots,** **+ 2 stalks sliced celery**	**Frozen corn**
Spice it up	**2 t lemon pepper seasoning**	**1 T Italian Seasoning**	**2 t of Spike or other seasoning mix**
	Simmer until vegetables are soft. Usually about 20 minutes.		

Depending on the base and ingredients you've chosen, you may need to add more spice. Making soup is a bit of an art form, and it may take a couple of tries to perfect your own personal recipe. Adding lemon juice or a dash of hot sauce can often take a soup from just okay to really delicious.

Lentil soup made with vegetable broth, 1 can lentils, sautéed onion, celery, carrots and Italian seasoning. Time from idea to table? 25 minutes.

The Big Salad

Yes, vegans get teased about only eating salad, but who cares if it's a great one?

Choose a Base	**Romaine Lettuce, chopped**	**Baby Spinach**	**Spring Mix**
Give it Substance	**Garbanzo, Black or Kidney Beans** *The canned version...rinsed and drained.*	**Edamame** *Purchase the shelled kind and prepare according to package directions.*	**Grilled Avocado and Tomato** *Put slices in a hot skillet and brown on each side.*
Choose Some Toppings	**Pepitas** *toasted/shelled pumpkin seeds*	**Sliced Olives**	**Wasabi Peas**
	Cherry tomatoes	**Diced Cucumbers**	**Shredded Carrots**
	Sliced Red Bell Pepper	**Sunflower Seeds**	**Corn**
Make a Dressing	In a separate bowl, whisk together one set of the following ingredients:		
	1 T Dijon Mustard **1 T Balsamic Vinegar** **2 T Olive Oil**	**1 T Soy Sauce** **1 T Rice Vinegar** **1 T Olive Oil** **1 T Maple or Agave Syrup** **¼ t Powdered Ginger**	**Juice of 1 lemon** **1 T Olive Oil** **Salt and Pepper**

Spinach salad topped with black beans, corn, black olives and grilled tomato and avocado. Salt and pepper added with a squeeze of lime. Time from idea to table? Less than 10 minutes.

Stuffed Spuds

Baked potatoes taste amazing. Especially if you top them well.

Prep the Base	**Baked Potato** *To cook in the oven: Scrub a potato, wrap with foil, bake at 350 for 1 hour or until soft.* *To cook in the microwave: Scrub a potato, wipe skin with oil and pierce it with a fork to create a steam vent, microwave for 5 minutes, then turn over and microwave for another three minutes. If not soft, microwave in 1 minute bursts until done.*		
Choose Some Toppings	½ can of Vegetarian Chili	Kidney, Black or Garbanzo Beans	Sliced Black Olives
	BBQ Sauce	Sliced green onion	Leftover curry or taco filling
	Corn or Green Peas	Tahini Dressing	Vegan Margarine and Tofutti's Better than Sour Cream

If you want a creamy taste to top the potato and don't have access to vegan margarine or vegan sour cream, try making tahini dressing. Tahini can be found in most large grocery stores in the ethnic or gourmet section. It is sesame paste and is a staple in Greek and Middle Eastern cooking.

Here is the recipe for tahini dressing:

In a blender or food processor combine: ¼ cup tahini, juice of 2 lemons or limes, 1 T olive oil, ¼ cup water, and ¼ t each salt and black pepper. Blend until creamy. Refrigerate any extra. The dressing will get thicker in the refrigerator. It keeps for about 4 days.

Oven baked potato filled with black beans, corn, peas, sliced black olives and topped with tahini dressing. Salt and pepper added to taste. Time to bake potato? 1 hour. Time to make tahini dressing and assemble/heat black beans, corn and peas? 10 minutes.

Vegan Breakfast

In American culture, one of the most difficult meals to eat vegan is breakfast. It is the one place where vegan convenience foods like soy yogurt, frozen vegan waffles and vegan sausage can come in really handy. But if you don't have access to these types of foods, no worries. There are still plenty of vegan breakfast ideas for you to grab on the go.

- Toast with hummus, peanut or almond butter.

- Granola with almond or soy milk. (See recipe in the snack section if you want to try making your own.)

- Smoothies. (See recipe in the snack section.)

- Peanut butter and banana sandwich.

- Oatmeal or other hot cereal with maple syrup. (Whole oats are simple to cook in a rice cooker. Just put in equal parts whole oats and water, then press the button and walk away. It takes about 15 minutes.)

- Sliced bagel with avocado smashed on it like cream cheese. (You can also add sliced red onion, sliced tomato and capers to dress it up.)

- Baked sweet potato.

- Raisin toast.

- Breakfast burrito made from a flour tortilla, refried beans and fried potatoes.

Pack a snack.

As a teen, you probably eat on the go...a lot. Whether you need things you can pack to get through your busy schedule or simply need to take something to a social event where there may not be anything on the menu for you, it helps to plan ahead.

Because plant-based foods are processed more quickly than meat and dairy, packing snacks will also help keep you fueled through the day between meals.

This section has recipes that you can make ahead, but if you don't have that much time, consider this list of "grab and go" snacks:

- Handful of almonds or other nuts.

- Peanut butter and crackers (homemade...skip the artificial ingredients in the premade kind).

- Vegan snack bars. Lara bars and Kind bars are available at most major supermarkets.

- Celery or carrot sticks with hummus.

- Box of raisins or other dried fruit.

- A banana with a packet of nut butter. (You can make your own "packet" with a baggie.)

- Quick guacamole made from mashing 1 avocado with a couple of tablespoons of salsa. Add lemon juice to keep it from turning brown.

- Popcorn.

- Edamame (Purchase frozen, prepare according to package directions, add salt and keep in baggies in the refrigerator.)

- Frozen grapes. (Rinse grapes and put in a baggie to freeze overnight so they will be ready to go the next morning.)

Granola

Granola is super simple to make...plus you can make it in volume. (It freezes well if you make too much.)

Stir together in a large bowl:

- 6 cups quick oats

- 6 cups old fashioned rolled oats

- 1/2 cup sugar or agave (if using agave mix in with wet ingredients instead)

- 2 t salt

Then throw in ¼ c vegetable oil and mix completely.

In a separate bowl combine:

- 1-1/2 cups water

- 2 t vanilla

Pour liquids into dry ingredients, mixing just enough to moisten evenly. Spread granola out evenly onto two large cookie sheets and bake at 250° stirring every 20 minutes or set oven to "warm" and leave overnight.

Remove from oven and allow granola to cool in pan, then store in baggies or other sealed container.

Change it Up	Apple Granola	Fruit and Nut Granola	Maple Granola
	Core and finely chop two large apples. Mix apples in with granola before baking. They will dry with the granola.	Before cooking, add ¾ cup chopped nuts of your choice. AFTER granola is baked add ¾ cup of your favorite dried fruit like cranberries, raisins, or chopped dates.	Leave out the sugar from the dry ingredients and add ½ cup maple syrup to the liquid ones.

In addition to being a quick to pack snack, granola makes a great vegan breakfast cereal when served with almond, soy or coconut milk.

Bean Dip

Bean dip is full of protein and can be great when you want a high protein snack.

It can be served with tortilla chips, pita chips, sliced veggies (like carrots, zucchini or cucumber) and/or crackers. You can also make your own pita chips by cutting flour tortillas into fourths and crisping in the oven at 350^0 on a piece of foil or a cookie sheet.

	Garbanzo Beans *1 can, rinsed and drained.*	Cannellini or Great Northern Beans *1 can, rinsed and drained.*	Black Beans *1 can, rinsed and drained.*
Choose a Base			
Add Flavor	**Juice of ½ a lemon or lime.** **1 clove fresh garlic, minced.** **1 ½ T tahini** **½ t salt** **2 T olive oil**	**1 clove fresh garlic, minced.** **½ t salt** **2 T olive oil** **2 T fresh rosemary**	**Juice of ½ a lemon or lime.** **2 T salsa**
Mix It Up	**Mash with a potato masher or a fork.**	**Put in a food processor and blend using the mixing blade.**	**Blend with an immersion blender.**

Bean dip made with Great Northern Beans, rosemary, garlic, olive oil, salt and pepper processed in a food processor. Time from idea to table? 7 minutes.

Simple Salsa

Put 2 – 3 tomatoes in a glass bowl with 1 – 2 fresh jalapeños with stems and seeds removed.

(Be sure to wash your hands with soap after that part because if you forget and touch your eye it really stings!)

Cover the bowl with a glass plate or glass lid and microwave for 3 – 4 minutes. (Enough for the tomatoes to split their skins).

Remove with a potholder (because the glass will be hot) and dump the mixture into a blender with a few shakes of salt from a shaker.

Pulse 2-3 times until it is "salsa" consistency, but stop before it gets too liquidy.

Guacamole

Guacamole is simply mashed avocadoes with vegetables in it. Try chopped tomatoes, onion, jalapeño, and cilantro. Then mix in some salt and the juice of a lemon to keep it from turning brown.

For really quick guac, just mash up an avocado with some salsa.

While you can always buy ready-made salsa and guacamole the homemade versions are much tastier and skip the preservatives. Besides, your friends will be impressed.

Smoothies

Smoothies are great for breakfast or an afternoon snack. They are also pretty portable when poured into a cup with a lid or poured into a bottle saved from some commercial drink and reused. Select from the ingredients below, throw in a blender and blend until smooth. Oh, and you might want a straw.

Choose a Base	1 cup fruit juice	1 cup soy or almond milk	1 cup water
Add the magic ingredient	1 frozen banana		
Give it flavor	1 cup frozen berries, any kind	1 cup frozen peaches	1 cup frozen mango
Optional: add extra nutrients	1 scoop protein powder (soy, rice or hemp)	1 cup fresh spinach *(once it goes through the blender with the other ingredients, you won't taste it)*	1 T cocoa or carob

Bananas just need to freeze overnight, but you may want to keep a large plastic bag in your freezer filled with bananas so that you will always have them whenever you want a smoothie.

Side note: frozen bananas are delicious all by themselves and make a great vegan "ice cream pop."

Pink smoothie made with vanilla almond milk, frozen banana and frozen strawberries. Chocolate smoothie made with vanilla almond milk, frozen banana, frozen strawberries, fresh spinach and cocoa powder.

Don't Stir Fruit Cobbler

If you have to put a dessert together without a lot of effort, this one is crazy simple.

Choose an Oil	½ cup coconut oil	½ cup vegetable shortening	½ cup vegan margarine
Put the oil in a 9 x 13 baking pan then heat in a 400° oven until melted.			

Make the batter	1 cup sugar 1 cup + 2T flour 2 t baking powder 3/4 cup almond milk		

Sift together the dry ingredients in a mixing bowl, then add the almond milk and stir until it forms a batter. Pour the batter evenly over the melted oil in the baking pan but,

DON'T STIR!

The hot oil will begin to cook the batter and create the crust as you pour it in.

Layer on the fruit	2 cups frozen berries, any kind	4 - 5 diced apples	1 20oz can of sliced peaches with half the juice.
Bake at 400° for 30 to 45 minutes.			

Let the cobbler "set" about 10 minutes once it is done baking.

Recipe in photo doubled to feed a larger group. Cobbler made with coconut oil, 2 cups of frozen blueberries and 2 cups of frozen raspberries.

Learn new stuff.

When I first became vegan and started reading vegan cookbooks, I got overwhelmed with the amount of ingredients I'd never heard of before. If you live in a big city, you can probably find most of these at the grocery store. If not, you can get them from a local health food store or order online. (Not that you need any of them, but as you continue to develop your cooking skills, they are fun to try.)

Nutritional yeast or "nooch."

First of all, the name 'nutritional yeast' is just gross. Vegan cookbook author Isa Chandra Moskowitz started calling it "nooch" and that has somehow caught on. It is a good source of vitamin B12, but that's not the main reason that vegans love it. The main reason is that it has a salty, buttery flavor that is great sprinkled over baked potatoes, pasta, popcorn and other foods. It is also the main ingredient in a lot of recipes for vegan cheese sauces. You can purchase it at health food stores. It is usually shelved near the supplements and protein powders.

Seitan.

Seitan—pronounced say-tahn—is basically wheat gluten that has been mixed with vegetable broth, kneaded into a dough and cooked. When that happens it has a "meat like" texture and is high in protein. While you can find recipes to make seitan with ingredients you can get at your local grocery store, at health food stores you can buy it pre-prepared. A word of caution...many people have gluten sensitivity. If that is the case for you, you may want to skip this one.

Tempeh.

Tempeh—pronounced tem-pay—is sold in patties. It is firm and has an almost nutty flavor. It is made from slightly fermented soybeans and the commercial brands available mix in other grains and sometimes flavors. It is high in protein and calcium and is great for adding into dishes when you want something more substantial than just veggies. Try slicing into strips and cooking it in the oil for the Tex-Mex, Asian and Italian recipies.

Braggs Liquid Aminos.

Bragg's Liquid Aminos is a liquid protein concentrate, derived from soybeans, that contains 16 amino acids. You can use it in food as a flavoring—like soy sauce. It also comes in a spray bottle. I love spraying it on popped popcorn. (It makes the nooch I sprinkle on stick.)

Agave Nectar.

Agave nectar comes from the agave plant—the same cactus that gives us Tequila. The flavor is sweet without the distinctive flavor that maple syrup has. It is a good replacement for honey or granulated sugar and is especially good in hot drinks.

Quinoa.

Quinoa—pronounced keen-wah—is an ancient grain that is popular in South America. The small seeds are cooked—like rice—and it has a mild, nutty flavor. You can cook it with vegetable broth instead of water to make it more savory. Serve quinoa as a side dish by itself, or mix in other ingredients like caramelized onions, chickpeas, raisins, olives, and/or dried cranberries to make a hearty quinoa salad. (It is usually recommended to rinse the quinoa before cooking because it can have a bitter taste if you don't.)

Texturized Vegetable Protein (TVP).

TVP is a meat substitute made from soy. You can often find it in the bulk bins at the health food store and there are boxed varieties at many grocery stores. Because it is dehydrated, TVP needs to have water or vegetable broth added and be allowed to sit for about 10 minutes to reconstitute. TVP has a similar texture to ground meat when cooked and works well when it is mixed into other things such as: soups, stews, chili, casseroles or spaghetti sauce.

Nori, Dulse, Kombu and Wakame.

These are sea vegetables that are widely used in Asian cooking. They are flavorful, full of minerals and a great source of chlorophyll. Nori is sold flavored as a snack. You may recognize it because nori sheets are used to create the rolls in sushi. Vegans often add a strip of kombu or wakame to the cooking water of rice, beans or soups to give flavor. Dulse is used as a condiment and can be sprinkled on foods. Try it on a baked potato to replace the bacon bits.

Eat out.

It helps to have a game plan when eating out.   Most Asian and Indian restaurants have good vegan options, but here are ideas on what to order when you are at restaurants that are not as vegan-friendly.

Steak Houses. Go for the baked potato which you can dress with steak sauce. Also look at the sides for grilled or steamed vegetables and salads. At high-end steak houses, the chef is usually familiar with special orders, so don't be afraid to ask if they have vegan options that simply aren't listed.

Mexican Restaurants. Try filling tortillas with guacamole and pico de gallo. (If the restaurant offers 'table side' guacamole, it is the freshest and the best. Look for entrees like veggie fajitas or spinach enchiladas (ask if they can give you a green sauce and leave off the cheese). It is doubtful that the beans and rice will be vegan, but you can ask. Depending on the restaurant, they might be.

Sandwich Shops. While most chains have a vegetarian option, few have good vegan options. Order the veggies you like and have them add sliced avocado or hummus (if they have it) to make it feel more like a meal. Skip the soup because it probably has a beef or chicken base.

BBQ. Get a baked potato and top with catsup and/or hot sauce. Load up on pickles and peppers. (If you are lucky they will have a salad bar.)

Greek Restaurants. Try falafel, dolmas, tabouli, hummus or baba ganoush with pita.

Italian. Order pasta with a tomato sauce, marinara sauce, olive oil and garlic sauce or try vegetable pizza without cheese. Minestrone soup is also typically vegan, but recipes vary by restaurant so it is a good idea to ask. Some bruschetta's are vegan also.

Fast food. By far, this is the hardest, but if you absolutely can't avoid it check to see if the chain has a baked potato, vegetarian beans for a burrito, salad or just get the French fries. Many chains have a vegetarian patty option for their burgers, so be sure to ask. (At the very least, if enough vegans ask, they may consider adding the option.)

Peta.org has a list of vegan options by restaurant chain, which is a great resource.

Have the Conversation.

You don't need your family to make the change with you, but it helps if they are supportive.

Be strategic in your conversations with them and make sure all are done with a great deal of respect and kindness. It is easy to let passion override judgment in this. After all, we are excited about it and probably talk about it way too much. If this is a new idea for your family, give it some time. A year spent living out your conviction showing your family the same compassion you are showing for animals will gain a lot more ground than a few intense, emotional conversations that hurt feelings and make people feel guilty.

Here are some answers to pushback you are likely to get:

Where do you get your protein?

You don't need meat to have muscle. Consider that elephants have incredible muscle mass and are vegetarian. Vegans get protein through the combination of legumes (beans, lentils, peas, soy) and whole grains (rice, wheat, breads, pasta). Other sources include nuts and surprisingly spinach and broccoli. Note that pinto beans have only slightly less protein than meat, but with no saturated fat or cholesterol.

But, humans are meant to eat meat...

Usually people will point out that we have forward pointing eyes and four canine teeth, yet they ignore that we have long folding intestines that allow for food to move slowly through our digestive system so that our bodies can absorb as many nutrients as possible before the food is passed. Animals that eat meat usually have short intestines because meat may contain pathogens and must be processed quickly. Also, we lack the proper PH in our stomach acid to digest meat properly without thorough cooking. An animal that eats meat has a stomach PH of around 1, but plant-eating animals have a PH of 4-5—which is what human beings have.

Don't you need milk?

Humans are the only animals that drink milk beyond infancy and then we drink milk which is designed for baby cows. You might be surprised to find out that human breast milk is only 5% protein.

Eating vegan is expensive.

If you purchase prepackaged vegan food, that can be true. But the recipes in this book are designed around basic ingredients like whole grains and legumes, which are substantially less expensive than purchasing meat.

The vegan lifestyle isn't healthy.

This part is up to you. After all, you could sit on the couch playing video games and eating potato chips and still be strictly vegan. How well you take care of your body with your nutrition and activity level will reflect on how your family and friends perceive your choices.

But, if you need to answer the question before you've had a chance to live that out, you may be interested to know that the leading cause of death in the United States is heart disease and studies show that diets high in red meats and saturated fat increase the risk. Conversely, diets high in whole grains, fresh fruits and vegetables decrease it.

But you are too young...

Learn to be gracious and take the concerns as caring, but know that if you are old enough to cook, you are old enough to live vegan. And, if you do a great job of it, you won't stress the people whose job it is to feed you. In fact, you might find yourself cooking for the rest of your family and influencing their choices, too.

More stuff...

If you are this far into the book, you are doing great, because the hardest part is figuring out what to eat. These are other things I wish I'd known in the beginning:

Take a B12 supplement. If we lived in a perfect world, eating food picked daily from nutrient-rich soil we probably wouldn't need to take supplements. B12 is the one that vegans get critically low on so it isn't optional. The sublingual ones dissolve under the tongue and are easy to take. Consider a good multivitamin with iron just to make sure all the bases are covered.

If you give up meat, you also have to limit sugar. This is a tough one. Most of us have way too much processed sugar in our diets and without the heavy proteins in meat to balance them out, you can really mess up your blood sugar and metabolism if you drop the meat but keep eating the sugar. You can still have natural sugars like fruit, maple syrup, sucanat or agave, but the processed kind will mess you up. (I discovered this one through experience.)

The less processed, the better. Think of it like this: an apple is nature's perfect source of fuel for our body. Bake it, and it loses some of the enzymes that fuel us, but still tastes great. Make it into applesauce by adding sugar and sitting it in a jar on a shelf for months and it is a little less great. Artificially make apple flavor and add green dye to make "apple candy" and we've lost the plot.

Read labels. There are animal products in foods you might not be aware of like gelatin (animal skin, ligaments, bones and sinews), glycerin (animal fat), rennet (calf stomach), lecithin (from animal tissues), and pepsin (enzymes gathered from pigs stomachs). If you are making the change for health reasons in addition to a passion for animals, then you aren't only reading for animal products (sometimes only listed as "natural flavorings") but you are also looking to eliminate preservatives and artificial colorings.

My kitchen is one of my favorite places. It is where I get to introduce friends to delicious plant-based meals.

From the author

I didn't start out as your most likely vegan. Instead, I grew up on baloney and cheese in the heart of cattle country. In my 20's, I worked for an educational consultant that was vegetarian and I remember thinking that I could never eat like she ate. But the more time I spent with her as she shared her meals and favorite restaurants, the less difficult and more appealing it seemed.

At first I thought of becoming vegetarian as a radical move to help fight my family history which included diabetes, high blood pressure and heart disease. I dropped red meat, then chicken, then dairy. I started reading authors like Marilu Henner and David Wolfe and cleaned out preservatives and artificial ingredients from my kitchen. At the time, it was all about health. It wasn't until later, when I read *Vegan Freak* by Bob and Jenna Torres that I considered the ethics of it. The book delved into factory farming practices, and once I knew about it, I couldn't "un-know" it. I felt I had a decision to make.

A big struggle for me in making the transition was learning how to think differently. For example, what was I supposed to do about shoes? What kind of purse should I carry? Could I give away my leather coat? Did it really count if I grabbed a cookie at work without checking ingredients? What if I went on a business trip and there was nothing on the menu for me?

I've learned to be patient with myself and realize that I can't get to where I want to go if I am obsessing on the things I haven't figured out yet. A piece of advice I read once—and I really wish I remember who said it—is "Vegan makes a great lifestyle, but it makes for a terrible religion." Lifestyle changes are a process. You won't get it perfect all the time. It helps to remember that every step you take toward a kinder lifestyle counts. What you are doing and why you are doing it matters.

I wish you the best on this journey and I hope you'll keep exploring. There are a lot of wonderful people out there on this path, and I'm thrilled that you are one of them.

- Cathy Hutchison

41143856R00027

Made in the USA
Charleston, SC
21 April 2015